Florence Nightingale

Lucy Lethbridge

Illustrated by Karen Donnelly

With historical advice from the
Florence Nightingale Museum, London

Internet links

For links to websites where you can find out more about Florence Nightingale, go to the **Usborne Quicklinks Website** at www.usborne-quicklinks.com and type the keyword "florence".

The recommended websites are regularly reviewed and updated but please note, Usborne Publishing is not responsible for the content of websites other than its own.

Series editor: Lesley Sims
Designed by Russell Punter
and Natacha Goransky

First published in 2004 by Usborne Publishing Ltd.,
Usborne House, 83-85 Saffron Hill, London
EC1N 8RT, England.
www.usborne.com

Printed in China. UE.
First published in America in 2005.

Contents

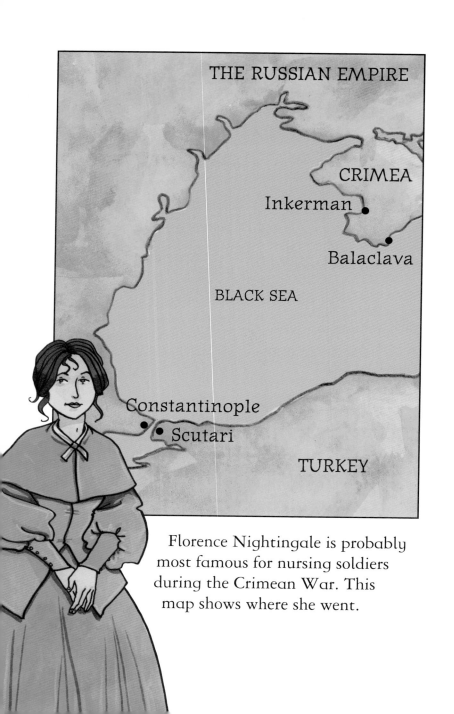

THE RUSSIAN EMPIRE

CRIMEA

Inkerman

Balaclava

BLACK SEA

Constantinople

Scutari

TURKEY

Florence Nightingale is probably most famous for nursing soldiers during the Crimean War. This map shows where she went.

Chapter 1

A defiant daughter

One hundred and fifty years ago, in the days of Queen Victoria, hospitals were so dirty that people came out much sicker than when they went in. Many didn't come out at all.

Patients used the same sheets and some even shared beds. No one knew there was a link between dirt and disease, so the floors stayed covered in filth and insects crawled over everything. As for the nurses...

...they were usually drunk, unwashed old women who knew nothing at all about medicine.

But one woman was to change everything. Her name was Florence Nightingale and she developed modern nursing. She was also the first English girl to be named Florence. Her mother – who liked the name – christened her after the city in Italy where she was born in 1820.

Florence's sister, who was two years older, wasn't so lucky. She was born in Naples, so their parents called her Parthenope, the city's name in Greek. No wonder the family always called them Parthe and Flo.

The Nightingales were incredibly rich – so rich that William Nightingale, the girls' father, could afford to spend his days reading in the library.

The girls' mother, Fanny, was much more sociable. What she liked doing most was holding dinner parties. When they first met, William showed her Lea Hurst, his vast house in northern England. Its huge windows looked out over rolling green hills.

But Fanny didn't like it.

Only fifteen bedrooms? That's far too small!

"Where will all our guests stay?" she complained. So William bought Embley Park, which was even larger, and closer to London.

The two houses were always filled with people, especially uncles, aunts and cousins, of whom they had dozens. There were cooks, maids, undermaids, footmen, gardeners, the butler and a housekeeper too.

But no matter which noisy house they were living in, the girls spent every day studying Greek, Latin, French, history, mathematics and philosophy with their father.

Flo adored her lessons, listening eagerly as he recited verbs, or nodding in agreement as he discussed a civil war. Parthe preferred painting.

Florence grew up pretty, clever and obsessed with keeping things neat. But she began to question her life. While she loved her family dearly, she didn't like the fact they were so rich.

Fanny often took her daughters to visit the poor in their village. She and Parthe sat up proudly in their shiny carriage, enjoying the admiring glances they received. Florence sank back into her seat, feeling guilty.

The people they visited lived in dark, damp rooms, were often sick and always hungry.

Parthe and Fanny went out of a sense of duty, but Florence passionately wanted to help. Her mother would distribute fruit from their greenhouses. Sometimes, she gave the villagers clothes and money as well. Then the three would return home, with Fanny already thinking of other things.

But while she and Parthe were planning their latest dinner party, Florence's mind would be back in the dank, stuffy cottages, remembering the hopeless faces she had left behind.

"We should do more!" she burst out, one day. "How can it be right that some people are starving, when we have so much food we throw it away? And why do we have two houses when so many people have nothing?"

Fanny frowned. "Really Florence," she scolded. "That's how the world is. It's not for you to question it."

Fanny worried when Florence spoke like this. She didn't mind her visiting the poor and sick occasionally, but she realized she would have to discourage Florence from going too often. After all, she might catch something.

Besides, Fanny wanted Flo and Parthe to marry the most dashing and wealthy men she could find, so they too could hold dinner parties in their own huge houses.

Parthe thought this an excellent idea. She and her mother spent most of their time thinking about where the sisters might meet their future husbands.

They spent the rest of the day arranging flowers, sewing intricate cushion covers and sitting in their drawing room, waiting for suitable gentlemen to visit.

13

"Come on Flo," snapped Parthe. "Take your nose out of that book. No man will want to marry a dusty old scholar!"

But Florence didn't think she wanted to get married. In fact, she thought that a life of nothing but dinners and flower-arranging sounded duller than ditchwater.

"Don't you want more?" she asked Parthe. "Wouldn't you rather have a job, where you can help people who need you?"

Parthe laughed and shook her head. "Whatever for?" she replied. "It sounds horrible."

Fanny could only sigh and pray her younger daughter would come to her senses.

"I can't spend my life just thinking about clothes and husbands," Florence whispered fiercely to herself. "I won't."

Chapter 2

The voice of God?

As the months went by, Florence grew more and more unhappy. She spent hour upon hour in her bedroom, dreaming of escaping her family. She was determined to do something worthwhile with her life.

Sometimes she thought she might like to marry one day... until she remembered what that meant. When Florence was growing up, rich married women had no choice but to stay at home, taking care of their husband and children.

Florence would retreat into her own world, her head full of daydreams of what might be. More than anything in the world, she wanted to work. To Fanny's fury, she started spending all her spare time with the poor in the village.

She risked catching terrible illnesses, by staying for hours by their bedsides, but Florence didn't care. Patiently, she sat holding their hands. She brought them baskets of fresh food and even little gifts.

Then, at seventeen, Florence had an experience that changed her life. She heard a voice in her head, the words as clear as if the speaker was standing beside her.

You must use your life to do good in the world.

Florence was convinced she had heard God. She was equally convinced that she should do as He asked – no matter how much fuss her family made. And, thought Florence with a sigh, they were bound to make a fuss.

The other problem was, she had no idea how she could help. Before she could do anything about it, Florence was swept up with rest of the family and taken on an extended tour of Europe. They journeyed along bumpy roads that were little more than tracks, staying in grubby roadside inns.

But when they reached the cities, they stayed in the best hotels and enjoyed a whirl of socializing. Florence seemed to blossom – her good looks and long, glossy hair attracted admiring glances from everyone.

As Fanny watched
the young men lining up to
dance with her beautiful daughter,
she sighed with relief. Perhaps,
at last, Florence would be happy to
settle down.

She was wrong — the old Florence
hadn't gone completely. While the rest
of the family was content simply
visiting galleries, Florence was writing
notes on everything they saw. She even
gathered statistics on operas.

The Nightingales moved on, from Italy to Switzerland. Their hotels were luxurious but Florence couldn't help noticing the desperate poverty on the streets. Her diaries were soon crammed with descriptions of the miserable life of the poor.

When the family finally returned to England, Fanny was ready to spring her daughters on London society. But Florence didn't want to attend one more ball. Every day, she heard the secret voice in her head.

"...use your life to do good."

It echoed around and around, until she felt dizzy. She had spent the last two years simply wasting time and the guilt was unbearable. Longing for something to focus on, and fascinated by statistics, Florence decided she would study mathematics.

Fanny was incensed, but Florence found an unexpected ally in her Aunt Mai, William's sister. Not only did Mai invite her niece to stay, she got up at six in the morning to help Florence study.

"She should have advanced mathematics lessons," Mai told Fanny.

"She's coming home at once!" replied Fanny, horrified.

Fanny gave endless parties; Florence retreated into her own private world. She went to her mother's dances, but she also got up with the dawn to study in secret. To everyone else she was a dutiful daughter – though if they had looked at her closely, they might have seen the strain around her eyes.

Her only moments of peace came when she was visiting the poor and sick. And it was during one of these visits that it finally dawned on her what she should do with her life. She would become a nurse.

Chapter 3

Fighting Fanny

Florence's plan seemed impossible. Girls of her class just didn't get jobs, let alone one that meant working in a dirty hospital. To be a nurse would bring shame upon the entire family. Parthe went into hysterics whenever Florence even mentioned leaving. What could she do?

"I don't want a life of showing off," said poor Florence.

Her mother still hadn't given up

trying to marry Flo off and she certainly had plenty of admirers. Several men had fallen in love with her 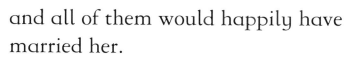 and all of them would happily have married her.

But, although Florence was tempted once or twice, she always refused.

"I have important work to do," she told her suitors gently. "I cannot be just a wife and mother."

"Oh Florence!" Fanny would cry, as yet another rejected man left the house. "Why must you make my life so difficult?"

"I only want to be free," Florence would murmur, under her breath.

She bought piles of books on medicine, sanitation and hospitals, read every one and made page after page of notes. Soon, she was an expert.

She started writing letters to papers and politicians, and found that there were people all over Europe who also wanted to make big changes in hospitals. Before long, she'd made many friends who thought as she did. She even learned about a hospital in Germany run by women of the Church.

You couldn't get more respectable than that.

But it made no difference to her family. The strain of being a dutiful daughter was just too much and, finally, Florence had a breakdown. Friends took her to Rome to recover.

While she was away, Florence met Sidney Herbert, a politician, and his wife Elizabeth, who became firm friends. More importantly, they encouraged Florence's desperate ambition to be a nurse.

Her stay in Rome left Florence in much better spirits, but returning to a despairing mother and sullen sister sank her into gloom once more. Was her life always going to be like this, she wondered.

Again friends took her away, this

time to Egypt. On the way back, they stopped in Greece, where Florence found an abandoned baby owl. Aside from her passion for studying, Florence loved animals — and here was a chance to care for something that needed her.

"I shall call you Athena," Florence whispered, stroking the owl's downy feathers. She made the owl a nest in the pocket of her dress and brought her back to England.

But Athena wasn't enough to lift her mood. Seeing her despair, her friends suggested she visit Kaiserwerth, the German hospital she had heard so much about. After two weeks there, Florence left inspired. She felt as if anything was possible.

The feeling didn't last. Back home, Parthe was hysterical and Fanny was incandescent with rage.

"Never mention that place to a soul," she spat at Florence. "Do you not care how you disgrace us?"

Florence stayed silent, but Fanny hadn't finished.

"You gallivant around the world without a thought for your sister. The worry is making her ill. You want to be a nurse? You can spend the next six months taking care of poor Parthe."

Florence had no choice. She was now thirty. She might as well have been six for all the independence she had. But the years of fighting for what she believed in were making her stronger.

Desperately, she asked her parents to let her return to Kaiserwerth and – finally – they agreed. At last, her life was beginning to move. On her return from Germany, she decided to ask her father to support her. To Fanny and Parthe's disgust, he did.

Florence was thirty-three when she had her first real chance. Elizabeth Herbert suggested her for the position of Superintendent at a hospital in London, for sick gentlewomen in distressed circumstances. Florence accepted and William even gave her an allowance.

"We've given up on you ever getting married, Flo," said Parthe, with a sigh.

Florence barely heard her sister, as she hurried around, packing Athena and a few clothes. Strange though it seemed to her family, Florence was truly happy. Now, she felt, her life would begin.

Chapter 4

Florence takes charge

Florence was appointed to organize everything in the hospital – and organize she did. Nothing escaped her notice, from hot water and food to fresh flowers. She replaced filthy bedlinen with crisp sheets, cleaned every ward and flung open every window. Florence was a breath of fresh air and the staff was shocked. Some she fired on the spot, but many others left of their own accord.

Once her hospital was running smoothly, Florence investigated other hospitals. She was writing notes on all the problems she came across when an epidemic hit London. Thousands of people, mostly in the poorest parts of the city, were struck down with cholera, a terrible disease caused by dirty water.

Florence couldn't do much for the cholera victims. But in her hospital, the patients were getting better and people noticed.

By now, it was 1854 and Britain was at war with Russia. British soldiers in the Crimea, a region by the Black Sea, were dying in their thousands — and more from sickness than battle wounds. A reporter from *The Times* had visited the battlefields and his reports shocked readers safe back in Britain. Conditions were terrible, he wrote: soldiers were left dying in the mud. Any who were taken to a hospital were likely to die even quicker. Florence's friend Sir Sidney Herbert now worked at the War Office. When he read the appalling reports, he knew there was only one thing to do. "We must send Florence to run a hospital," he declared.

Florence was overjoyed. "This is it! This is how I can do good," she thought, when the government asked her to travel to Turkey and the Crimea to take care of the soldiers. Surprisingly, even Fanny and Parthe approved. If she had to nurse, she might as well do it for her country.

First, Florence had to choose a team of women to take with her.

Florence decided to train the women herself, teaching them about hygiene and medicine. They would be the first trained nurses in the world and they would work at the soldiers' hospital at Scutari, in Turkey.

Florence chose her nurses carefully. They were neither too young, nor too old. She didn't want them running off with the soldiers, but she didn't want to have to take care of them either.

Then she designed a uniform – a plain dress with a white apron and a white cotton hat to keep hair out of the way. Rings and brooches were forbidden.

Everything was orderly, efficient and clean, exactly as Florence knew a hospital should be. Finally, she found thirty-eight nurses willing to join her. She was ready to go.

As they crossed Europe, Florence picked up extra supplies. After reading the newspaper reports, she didn't entirely trust the War Office. Much of the journey was by boat, and many of the nurses were seasick. But when the unfamiliar, magical landscape of Constantinople came into view, they forgot their sickness in wonder. Now they were eager to arrive and start work. They had no idea of what they were about to face. Even Florence, who thought she had seen people suffering in the worst conditions, was shocked.

It was like entering hell.

Chapter 5

Hell on earth

The hospital at Scutari was disgusting. It stank of blood and mud, old clothes and worse. Wounded soldiers lay on the ground, or on straw mattresses which were covered in dirt and infested with lice. The men hadn't washed for months and the only toilet was a hole outside. If they were too

weak to go outside, they went in the straw where they lay.

The men were caked with blood and lice crawled all over them. They were simply too weak to brush the lice away.

The hospital itself was an old barracks: four miles of filthy corridors filled only with thousands of suffering soldiers. There were no medicines, no bandages and no beds. There wasn't even a single table for the surgeons to operate on.

And while the nurses had been expecting a grateful welcome, they were greeted with resentment.

The army doctors didn't approve of Florence and were appalled by the idea of women on battlefields. A lady's place was at home. Besides, ordinary soldiers were brutes and expected to be tough.

"You want to treat the men like babies!" they snorted in disgust.

Florence saw she would have to tread carefully. At first, she was only allowed in the kitchen. So, relieved she had brought her own supplies, she cleaned it and made reviving beef tea.

For soldiers who were doubled up with stomach cramps, used to forcing down lumps of greasy boiled meat, she brought a taste of heaven.

But still the army officers refused to let Florence and her nurses nurse. It was a stalemate... until two battles, at Balaclava and Inkerman, sent an avalanche of casualties to Scutari. The doctors panicked and finally called Florence.

While her nurses began scrubbing the barracks, Florence walked from one end to the other, making a list of what she would need: everything.

Readers of *The Times* had donated money and Florence ordered food and clothes, pans, pillows, cups and candles. Alongside her nurses, she made up beds with clean sheets and filled huge jugs with hot water to wash the patients.

The hospital was transformed... but the death rate went up. Florence couldn't understand it. Then an epidemic swept the hospital, killing soldiers, nurses and doctors alike.

When the news reached London, the worried government sent health inspectors to investigate.

What they found shocked everyone. Not only had the barracks been built over sewers, but two dead horses were also blocking the pipes, polluting every drop of water. When the pipes were cleaned up, things began to improve.

Even the food changed for the better, when a famous French chef arrived and took over the kitchen. Meanwhile, Florence didn't stop, staying on her feet for twenty-four hours at a time.

Although always strict with her nurses, she was only ever kind and gentle to the soldiers and they all adored her.

At night she walked along the wards, listening to the invalids crying out in their sleep and soothing them. The men saw her lantern moving through the dark like a comforting angel and named her the Lady with the Lamp.

Though she couldn't stop and speak to – or even smile at – everyone, the men could lean out of their beds and kiss her shadow as she passed.

Sometimes Florence stopped and took their hands, or adjusted their pillows. Sometimes she whispered comforting words in their ear. Once, she saw a patient with the flaky skin disease, scurvy. Reaching into her pocket, she took out an orange.

"Eat this," she whispered. "It will help you get better."

Instead of eating it, the soldier put the orange under his pillow to remind him of the Lady with the Lamp. He kept it all his life even after it had dried out and gone black.

Florence persuaded the generals to put up a building for soldiers who were getting better – with puzzles, games and comfortable chairs. She even put flowers by the soldiers' beds.

"Pah!" said the generals. "Flowers

for men!"

Florence ignored them. She was convinced that beautiful things would help the men feel better. Soon, the Scutari hospital was running smoothly and, once more, Florence turned her attention to the other hospitals nearby. But she had pushed herself too hard. While visiting Balaclava, she collapsed with a fever.

For two weeks, she lay near death. Tossing and turning in her bed, she was drenched in sweat and shivering with cold at the same time. She returned to Scutari thin and pale, but determined to carry on.

To her disappointment, the clean,
efficient hospital she'd left was a
complete mess — and the nurses
and army doctors were too busy
squabbling to notice.

Florence was as single-minded as
ever, but she was too weak to cope.
Help came from an old ally, her
Aunt Mai, who set sail from England
at once.

Souvenirs of
Nurse
Nightingale

Mai left behind a country in the grip
of Florence fever. Souvenirs of Nurse
Nightingale were being made in their
thousands. Her supporters could visit a

display of Florence nursing the sick in Madame Tussaud's waxwork museum, in London. People even named a lifeboat and a racehorse after her.

Then a Nightingale Fund was set up to buy Florence a gift. So much money was donated, there was enough to establish a nurses' training school. And every single soldier contributed a day's pay.

Fanny was ecstatic and wrote to Florence to tell her how proud she was. But Florence was miserable. Although some soldiers had started going home, she was still fighting the generals and their prejudices, and her nurses argued constantly.

At long last, peace was declared. Florence waited until the last soldier had left Scutari before she and Mai headed home. Numerous parties were planned, but Florence wanted none of them. She crept home quietly, not even letting her family know.

Queen Victoria, delighted with Florence's hard work, sent her a magnificent brooch with thanks.

But Florence wasn't interested. All she could think of were the thousands of soldiers she hadn't been able to save, the thousands of boys left behind in Crimean graves.

Chapter 6

Fame

Florence came home to fuss and she hated it. Within days, she was drowning in fan mail. Fanny and Parthe, on the other hand, were delighted. Florence was famous! They had no idea why she didn't want the rewards of fame herself, but they were happy to enjoy them for her.

Florence had other things to think about. Working in Scutari had shown her how desperately army hospitals and the nursing profession needed to be reformed. Somehow, she was going to bring about the change. She just didn't know how...

...until Queen Victoria and her husband, Prince Albert, invited Florence to come to Balmoral, their castle in Scotland.

"That's an invitation you can't refuse," said Fanny, in awe.

Florence agreed – but for an entirely different reason.

Along with her best clothes, she packed notebooks bursting with facts and figures of the suffering she had seen. She was going to convince the Queen to support her quest for reform.

When Victoria and Albert saw the amount of research Florence had done and heard her forceful but quiet pleas, they were impressed.

Before long, a Royal Commission had been set up to investigate the health of the army, and Florence was working harder than ever. Fanny and Parthe – who still hadn't found a husband – sped to London offering help, although their help consisted mainly of lying around, moaning about the heat.

Florence stayed in her room, researching army barracks and hospitals all over London, and then writing reports on everything. She filled page after page with tables, graphs and charts of statistics – many of which she designed herself.

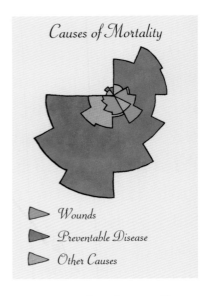

Causes of Mortality

▷ Wounds
▷ Preventable Disease
▷ Other Causes

Once again, Florence worked until she collapsed and once again Aunt Mai came to the rescue.

Fanny and Parthe were no help whatsoever, so Florence was delighted when they were distracted by the rich Sir Harry Verney. He had wanted to marry Florence, but when she refused him, he proposed to Parthe.

Parthe jumped at the chance. Fanny couldn't believe their luck. At nearly

forty years old, one of her daughters
was getting married. Immediately,
Fanny and Parthe began preparing for
the wedding.

Florence moved into a London
hotel, where she continued to
work from a sofa.

Chapter 7

Working flat out

Having done as much as she could with army hospitals, Florence moved on to ordinary ones. As always, she paid attention to the tiniest details, and wrote up her research in *Notes on Hospitals*. She followed it with *Notes on Nursing: what it is and what it is not*.

She covered everything, from the importance of fresh air, to a quiet and peaceful ward. "A nurse who rustles," she wrote, "is the horror of a patient."

She even discussed unexpected visitors. "Why... let your patient ever be surprised, except by thieves?"

"It's as good as a novel!" declared her good friend, Sir Sidney Herbert. The public agreed. *Notes on Nursing* became a best-seller.

Florence put her words into action and set up a training school for nurses. She interviewed every nurse herself and followed their progress, sending them flowers, books – and cake on their birthdays.

Then, quite unexpectedly, Sir Sidney died. Florence was overwhelmed with grief. She coped the only way she knew how, by burying herself in work. But it had the usual effect: she collapsed. This time, she was so ill, she didn't leave her sofa for six years.

But Florence had gained respect for her constant research and wide knowledge. Government officials began bombarding her with papers to draft or new problems to solve. She was asked to investigate workhouses – the Victorian dumping ground for the poor and sick; the state of the army in India and laws for the poor.

She was taken up with battles for reform, still bitter that Sir Sidney had died before they had finished with the army. To save her energy, she only saw people who came about work and even then she preferred them to send messages instead.

But, though she avoided people, she still loved animals, especially her cats. Haughty, regal creatures, with long, shining fur and glowing green eyes, they sprawled around her room, keeping her company.

And every morning, Florence would feed birds and squirrels at her window. She covered her fingers with butter and the sparrows would come and gently peck at them.

She might have stayed like that forever, working alone and shut away from the world. But then two things happened. First, the Nightingale Nursing School, which she had left to run itself, descended into chaos. Then her elderly parents grew sick and needed someone to care for them. Parthe proved no help in this at all.

Florence hadn't seen her parents for nearly ten years, but she decided to divide her time between them and the nursing school. Going back to where she had begun, organizing nurses and caring for William and Fanny, brought out Florence's gentler side. She even made friends with her sister.

After her parents died, Florence returned home to her house in London and went to bed. She hardly got out of

it for the rest of her life. She was soon
surrounded by thousands of papers
again, but this time they weren't pages
of graphs, but gossipy letters from
friends and nurses all over the world.

Florence was still a perfectionist,
but now, instead of the hospitals, it
was her home which had to be neat
and spotlessly clean. Above all, she
still abhorred attention. She didn't like
having her photograph taken and she

hated people to fuss. But when Queen
Victoria celebrated fifty years on the
throne, with her Golden Jubilee,
Florence's work formed a special
part of the exhibition.

Old soldiers who had been at Scutari
remembered the Lady with the Lamp
with tears in their eyes.

Gradually Florence became old and frail. As her eyes grew weaker, she could no longer read and write all day and into the night. Her window blinds were kept closed and Florence was left in the company of her beloved cats.

In 1907, she received her greatest tribute and hardly noticed. Edward VII had decided she should be the first woman to receive the royal Order of Merit. When his servant arrived with the medal, Florence barely woke up.

She died in her sleep in 1910, aged ninety. Right to the end, Florence wanted no fuss. After a quiet funeral, she was buried near her family in Hampshire.

Nurse Nightingale - My Life

May 12 1820 - I'm born in Florence, Italy.

1837 — I hear a voice telling me I must do good in the world.

1847 — While visiting Rome, I meet Sidney and Elizabeth Herbert.

1849 — Friends take me to Egypt and then Greece where I rescue an abandoned baby owl I name Athena.

1850 — I spend two fascinating weeks studying a hospital in Kaiserwerth, Germany.

1851 — A second visit to Kaiserwerth and the year Father finally accepts I should be a nurse. (Mother and Parthe grow hysterical.)

1853 — I become Superintendent of the Institute for the Care of Sick Gentlewomen in Distressed Circumstances, in London.

1854 — Britain, France and Turkey declare war on Russia. Sidney sends me to Scutari, in Turkey, to run a hospital for the soldiers.

1856 — Peace is declared in April, although I stay on in the Crimea until July. In September, Queen Victoria invites me to Balmoral.

1857 — I begin researching the state of the British Army's healthcare.

1858 — Parthe and Sir Harry Verney are married.

1859 — I publish Notes on Nursing, followed by Notes on Hospitals.

1860 — My Nightingale Training School for nurses opens.

1861 — My dear friend Sidney Herbert dies. I am overcome with grief.

1862 on — Burying myself in work I research India and workhouses.

1872 — I start taking care of my elderly parents.

1873 — I become more closely involved in running the training school.

1877-84 — I campaign for reforms in India.

1896 — I retire to my bed. Though I continue to work, from now on I never leave my bedroom.

1907 — Edward VII awards me the Order of Merit, though I sleep through the ceremony.

On August 13, 1910 Florence died peacefully in her sleep. She was buried with her family in Hampshire.